In the name of God, the Beneficent, the Merciful, without Him, I am nothing.

To my family and friends

*I love you dearly.
You have made me what I am.
Thank You.*

Life's Song
Copyright @ 2008

Second Edition: January, 2008

All rights reserved. No part of this book may be reproduced or transmitted in any form or by any means, electronic or mechanical, including photocopying, recording, or by any information storage and retrieval system, without written permission from the publisher, or author, except for the inclusion of brief quotations in a review.

International Standard Book Number: 978-0-9556847-0-8

In the name of God, the Beneficent, the Merciful, without Him, I am nothing.

Introduction

I'd like to thank you, the reader, for taking time to read this book. I hope it will inspire, and delight, and take you on a journey through life's up's and downs, trials and tribulations. This has been my dream, and now to finally see it come alive, I hope you realise your dreams.

I dedicate this book to my dear wife Rubbina, and my children, Yahya, Bilal and Alisha, my family and friends, who have stood by my through my life's song. A big thank you goes to the people I have known in my life, some have come and gone, some have left deep scars, but all have helped me to become who I am today. We are only a culmination of our past experiences, and to that I have no regrets, and so to some of you Saleem, Mila, I give you this special mention, for without you this book would never exist.

I started to write these words when I was about 15, and as you can tell from the different moods and styles through these words I have aged, both mentally and physically. Through my life it has been these words that I have captured some of my soul and essence, and through them reveal some of my feelings and dreams.

Words have become my freedom of expression, and through them you can realise the potential within yourself. The power to let your mind wander and dream, the power to think beyond the here and now, the thrill and excitement of loosing yourself among the words, becoming whatever dream and fantasy you may wish, believing it, experiencing it. It is through these words I have discovered many things about myself, some truth and some fiction, but a discovery of identity and expression. In a world where restrictions are everywhere, truly there is no restriction in the mind, and it is here in the words that you can find true freedom. That is where I found mine.

I have started with my very first piece I wrote. Written for a school "house" competition it has been these words that have defined me. From that young boy into the person I am today those words still cast a shadow of my youth, and the first sparkle of expression I have felt. So let's begin this journey of words. Prepare to free your mind and stir your soul.

Imran Umar

Words are not just expression, they are the freedom within us all !!!

Life's Song

Imran Umar

One Mans Future

The future seems dark,
No man can feel what I do,
The hope, the despair,
The dream that has died,
Only to be replaced by a nightmare,
I live my life on the edge,
The edge of what they call sanity,
But is it me who is really insane?

I know not the fate that lies ahead,
But the feeling of deep and total despair.
The lives of many who hide in fear,
In fear of what, no one knows,
I feel damned by the outside,
Cursed for what I believe in,
No one can know what this is like,
No one apart from those like me,
Those who live in fear,
But these are but a few,
Or so it seems!

Am I the only one left in this insane world?
One man alone in his fight for freedom,
Am I not a man as they are?
Why can't they see me for what I am?

A Minds Eye

Have you ever searched the deepest darkest depths of your mind?
Take a look through the darkness,
Stare hard into the fantasia of colours.
What lies in the darkness?

A yellow sun, that glows so bright upon hills of green and lakes so blue,
A towering castle that invites the warm glow of the oil burning lamps,
A knight in shining armour riding proud on his steed of silver,
Tales of days gone by and endless summers,
From which dusk was only the beginning.

Then back to reality you fall,
The hustling streets and busy lives,
Of men and women striving for their future,
They strive to make there dreams come true,
Yet why do this when they can too,
Just close their eyes like me and you,
And step into a mind's eye view.

A Tale Of Two Lovers

Two star-crossed lovers, destined to die,
Both Romeo & Juliet knew not why,
There deaths so sad yet so profound,
A famous story was that which was found.

Their love knew no binds of time,
Infinite in the words of rhyme,
Like the love between two lovers now,
that know not what the future may hold.

Yet struggles and tasks they face together,
Everyday their love growing stronger,
Forever, this pair will hope to live,
though they know this cannot be,
For death is certain in everything.

Yet they hold their love like the two before.
Till the ends of time and forever more.

A Teacher's Thoughts

"What's the point!", "How long now?", the thoughts go round the classroom.
"Not too long to go now" sighs the teacher.
"Right, homework time", "What shall I give them today?"
"I think exercise 3, it's easy to mark!"
"It's also easy for them".

"But what's the point, half of them won't do it"
"Better get the usual detentions ready"
"But it's not there fault, what are the parents viewing?"
"Sitting in front of that box, knowing not what their kids are doing".

"Roaming the streets, not a care in the world"
"Skinning up under the dim street lamps"
"While their parents don't care what they're up to"
"Just staring faces blank, mesmerised by the screen"
"Done your homework, occasionally they shout"
"Not knowing that their kids are out".

"And they expect their kids to grow up"
"To be doctors, and lawyers all good in the world"
"But where is their guidance, the home the first school?"
"It's not the kids fault, it's the parents who're the fools"
Brrring, Brrring, goes the bell.
"Well time to go kids, don't forget the homework, due in next fall"
"Well another day over but more to come".

My Angel

Good morning world! As the head appears,
For one so calm and so sincere,
Not knowing the troubles life may bring,
As she opens her eyes to a new world within.

All around her throughout her life,
She'll be surrounded by love and people she likes,
And I'll be there to protect her so,
And not let harm even near her soul.

For she is mine to raise and teach,
The value of life and what it brings,
To teach her good and what is right,
And not let her stray into the night.

Where darkness prevails and not just outside,
But in the hearts and minds of people disturbed,
But I will be there to hold her hand,
And keep her safe through this rough land,
For she is mine and will forever be,
My sweet angel for eternity.

Torn

Two personalities I have to keep,
For one so pure and one so sweet,
My heart she has captured, with words so pure,
And her intellect is one I simply adore.

But my mind it also lusts away,
For the other whose words are simply profane,
The animal in me would like to see,
Just how true her words could be.

But the one so lustful corrupts me so,
With thoughts of the pure that I wish I could show,
For the innocence and purity I would like to break,
And let the animal inside of me suddenly awake.

The lust for her I should not have,
But the other corrupts each hour at hand,
But the corruption I like for it turns me so,
To thoughts of the other so deep and so low.

But for now I will let the animal lie,
For the one so pure who I would not let die,
But the animal is strong and so I shall,
Release on the other who sees it so,
To wait and watch and let it grow.

Bomb

Through the darkness, in slumber he rests,
His dreams never endless,
The nightmares still haunt,
Of childhood memories once forgotten,
The cries of his sister and brother alike.

Torn apart from the world with a blistering light,
They had no warning of when it would strike,
And he stood and he watched, as the dark became light,
No noise was heard until later that night,
When the bomb hit a building not even in sight.

Trapped in the buildings he watched them all die,
With no regret he turned a blind eye,
Until now that is when all is astray,
But now is too late for the error of his way,
From now till death he will have to face,
The decision he made to let the bomb go that day.

Stolen Hearts

She blows my mind in everyway,
I would love for there to be a day,
When face to face one day we meet,
A day when we can feel the heat,
Of passion that burns inside me so,
For her I would love to go,
To the ends of the earth, till kingdom come,
My heart is stolen by this one.

But she is so far away,
That I'll probably never see that day,
When face-to-face we meet in heat,
And chest-to-chest we feel the beat,
Of our hearts together as one,
And longing of mine just like the sun,
That shines upon us everyday,
T'is like my passion that won't go away.

For now it's all a fantasy,
I dream of her to keep me sweet,
Until that day should ever come,
When we make love forever as one.

Natures Beauty

Shy is she though we've been known a while,
I sent her flowers, which are divine,
For her I show my innermost soul,
Yet she's to shy to display her all.

She understands not the longing I have,
That one day I'll see her beauty and be glad,
That I've known this person in my life,
And the impact she made just like a knife.

That cuts through my heart like a fiery blade,
For this person knows not this,
I wish she did and could see my bliss,
That I would have, should she show to me,
The beauty of nature that she be.

Deep Blue

In the darkest depths of the deepest seas,
Lives a world unknown to both you and me,
Full of riches and wealth of vigour and life,
And tales untold and forgotten in time.

The bluest seas are nice to see,
But the real treasure is in you and me,
To see what awaits us deep inside,
And face those fears and ghosts gone by.

To know the future and what it hides,
Is the scariest thing in the vast tides,
Of time and space we knew this is true,
The future awaits us, like the sea that is blue.

The oceans of time we cannot get back,
Make our futures more certain to that we adapt,
For like the oceans blue that change so true,
Like the passing of life and that which we knew.

So go find your ocean and make it your goal,
To stay true to your treasure, the one which you stole,
By wasting your life in the past sands of time,
Now look to the future and the oceans of mine.

A Childs Storm

The wind roars on this old winter's morn,
The bed feels cold and empty for this dawn,
I sit awake scared of what is to come,
I long for the blue skies and the sun.

The trees bend with the forces of nature,
Bowing for their life or so it seems,
I sit here quietly watching in the shadows,
Hoping it will get never closer.

For in this storm there may be a calm,
But will I live to see it, I feel the sweat in my palms,
This wind rips through houses will a powerful force,
And so what's stopping them to come for me of course.

I hide under covers thinking I will be safe,
But what about the rest? Where lies there fate?
The sky grows dark now, darker than before,
All I want to see is that calm after the storm.

And then like a flash a silence, so loud,
Not a whisper of the wind that was sweeping the ground,
I look up now to see a blue sky ahead,
Maybe the calm is here...or am I dead.

I look all around to see the destruction it made,
The forces of nature and the houses it's laid,
But safe was I, hid in my room,
And awake I am now to see all the doom.

Lights

Looking out through the dark of the night,
The lights of the streets flick on and off,
Like dancing fireflies that can be seen,
The dark skies become light with the beauty of these,
In all different colours they shimmer.

But not in the country for they cannot be found,
But in the cities and towns and all around,
The busy metropolis where people stay,
To light up there rooms when the dark of the day,
Sets in for the night and for hours to come.

But come dawn all that dances is a few moving cars,
While people are sleeping within the homes,
And no more dancing till nightfall returns,
When the fireflies will return to light up the dark,
And set things alight like the fire of my heart.

My Child

I see those eyes and they make me melt,
Nothing can describe the joys I felt,
That finally here a child of my own,
To love and to cherish and really take home.

So pure and so small my little one appears,
To see her smile only brings me tears,
The joy I feel is something so strong,
I know that she's mine and cannot do her wrong.

To cuddle and to hold for all of my life,
My little one will be safe like the hands of a knife,
To protect her and keep her safe and from harm,
I will do whatever I can with my wit and my charm.

I will work everyday just to keep her at bay,
Yet spend my whole life with her always at play,
For work is important to get what you need,
But without the love and attention her heart will surely bleed.

For the love of a father through those childhood years,
Nothing can replace them, not even with tears,
For time is so precious when they are so young,
That they grow up so fast with each rising of the sun.

And when it's those years where she's coming of age,
I'll be there for her, like the turning of a page,
A new chapter starting with new times ahead,
I will look after and protect her until I am dead.

Man

Through the dimly lit streets he makes his way,
Not stopping to take the time of the day,
With forceful steps, with a purpose in mind,
A desperate man with no past behind.

A shadow for company, no name to speak of,
a past left forgotten, lost in times love,
Just on his own in this world left unkind,
For now he runs away from his mind.

But there is no escape from the prison of mind,
But that's just a lie to bide the time,
Escape is possible in every way,
Just free your mind and drift away.

The shadows of the past will be there still,
To haunt you in your dreams, yet still,
The past is something you cannot change,
So look to the future for all will be clear,
But you need to stop running and to face your fears,
This is not easy but you'll find a way,
To free your mind the natural way.

No drugs do you need to get rid of this prison,
Just life and the past and all of its lessons,
So remember my friend as I leave the shadows tonight,
Free your mind and with that live your life.

Life's Song

I see the people in the streets,
With blank expressions, lost like sheep,
They follow each other in a melodious manor,
Like a swarm full of bees, not that it matters.

But why be a sheep or a slave to your mind,
When all you need is to take a little time,
Think of the things that have impacted your life,
A brother or sister or even a wife.

Take the futures hands now a lead them along,
And make an impact on someone else's song,
A song of their life is what it shall be,
And you help them write it for their eternity.

And there it shall stay in the accounts of man,
A song that you helped make true or to plan,
With a little note inside that says that it's true,
That you shaped the life of someone you knew.

And no longer will those sheep increase,
Nor the swarms of the bees shall ever decrease,
Because just like ours mind they will be free at last,
To sing out the songs you've helped write in the past.

Fantasy

Close your eyes and come with me,
On a journey full of fantasy,
Of kings and queens and jack rabbit tales,
And of castles and kingdoms that fly high or set sail.

Your fantasies are a powerful tool,
They shape you and mould you, just like in school,
For without fantasies your mind would die,
The imagination that you just let lie.

For without this tool you cannot survive,
Through some of the troubles you face through your lives,
For its imagination that keeps us sane,
Those creative cells within your brain.

Some time it's good to sit alone,
And let all those juices release their moans,
And let them create for they know best,
Until next time when you put them to rest.

My Love's Beauty

As I sit here in the darkness, my wife by my side,
I conjure up some magic words to get me through the night,
For as she sleeps my mind's awake,
With thoughts and ideas of what to write.

I see her sleeping so calm and so serene,
In the moonlight her beauty can be seen,
Like a silver lining upon clouds so high,
Her beauty shimmers all through night.

But the moonlight cannot compare,
With the beauty of hers and that of her hair,
The dark black strands that linger around,
Waiting for my touch so they can be found.

I always believed in fate and destiny,
But now truly believe she was meant for me,
Her smile brings to me joy everyday,
I'm glad she's mine and here to stay.

For I will love her for eternity,
And past that time if it's meant to be,
And in heaven again we shall meet,
Our promise forever for us to keep.

John Doe

The moonlight shines on the body so pale,
Yet another John Doe escaped from jail,
Only to find there's no where to go,
No loved one's for him to help him so.

But why did it have to come to this,
But the temptation for him was strong to resist,
And now look at him laying down there,
Not knowing or watching everyone stare.

At his cold naked body just lying around,
Somehow washed up on this lonely ground,
The ambulance comes but it's already too late,
Another Doe dead, such an unfortunate fate.

So sad is this world that we all live inside,
For someone to even think of suicide,
For even if he was accused of a murder most foul,
Death to him should not be his way out.

But for some this was better than spending the time,
Within four walls, with only their minds,
For the mind plays tricks even horribly so,
That death may be better then the taunting so low.

And as the mind continues to play its old tricks,
The sanity quickly starts to slip,
And then by now it is clear to see,
That the only way out was to be buried at sea.

So you see though the mind can give you advise,
It can also be there to destroy all that's nice,
Like the John Doe's before,
That escaped from the law.

Forever

I speak to her everyday,
With words so true and so sincere,
Some foul thoughts I would love to see,
Them all become a reality.

To see her flesh so soft and true,
Her nipples erect by the morning dew,
After a nights long of passion among the fields,
Our naked bodies the sun would reveal.

And I'd keep her warm all through that long night,
With whispers of words that needed no light,
For they would be powerful, and bright as day,
Filled with passion and love in every way.

And like a fairy tale we would live forever,
In the dreams of our future of us together,
And with each passing night that we sleep throughout,
Our love would grow stronger without a doubt.

Friends

All throughout our life we make many friends,
But only a few of them are there till the end,
Through all of your troubles and the trials,
They'll always be there for you all of the while.

They come in many in many forms and ways,
From a lifelong companion to a stranger far away,
But in common they all have the very same thing,
They care and protect you and friendship they bring.

For where would we be without our dear friends?
Alone in a gutter somewhere until the very end,
They help and inspire us throughout our lives,
To do better in life and take all of its trials.

For friends like this are so hard to find,
But if you do then keep this in mind,
For life may be tough but it's always nice to know,
That you will have this friend come sun, rain or snow.

Life's Love

*Her name so lovely though I know not why,
Her voice full of passion that I have to sigh,
When I hear her first word to me every day,
Just glad that she's there to talk my way.*

*I hate when the days come and she is not there,
My heart gets so jealous knowing not where,
She may be around with other friends so,
I shouldn't be jealous that's an evil so low.*

*But for some reason she makes my heart a flutter,
With the words that she says, they make me stutter,
I think about her all of the time,
And think of some words just to put into rhyme.*

*For my poetry she likes which makes me proud,
That everyday I wish I could sing so loud,
My love for her through all its divinity,
And confess it to her for all of eternity.*

*But my love for her that grows so strong,
Cannot be told to the one that I long,
For her happiness to me is all that I need,
As I care for this person and so I will lead.*

*My thoughts of her I have everyday,
Why has she captured me in this way?
And yet she knows not the pain that I feel,
When she talks to another or goes for a meal.*

*The jealousy inside me just wants to rage,
And be set free for life and out of this cage,
But I should know that her feelings for me,
Go no deeper than a wound on my skin.*

Though some poems I write with her in mind,
It's one of life's quirks that I should be left behind,
While she chooses another and friends are just we,
And I care for her happiness too much for her to see,

That all of this pain it just cuts like a knife,
That one day she may be out of my life,
And no longer will I enjoy our everyday chats,
It'll just be me again watching my back.

While she lives her life in true happiness,
Not knowing my life and the sadness,
But I will be happy for her as I truly do care,
About this one in my life who knows not I'm there.

Night Creatures

Darkness surrounds me everywhere,
Not a single light can be seen,
What are those patterns that I see?
Merely shapes and figure from my imagination.

The dark seems to scary for me,
My mind plays tricks that seem so haunting,
Those figures in the dark, I can see them take shape,
Those night creatures I can feel them awake.

It not a comfortable feeling being watched,
Especially by things that I cannot see,
But I know they are there and it scares me so,
For every night I can hear them when I turn out the lights.

The whispers they make, too silent to hear,
But I know they are talking while they stare,
Those eyes they glint, though no light is present,
There voices are heard even if they are silent.

But why do they watch me in the still of the night,
Why are they there when I turn out the light?
To haunt me with things I better not dream of,
For if I'm awake I'd rather not know them.

The Writer

Everyday I seem to seek,
The one that's pure and oh so sweet,
For presents for her I cannot buy,
But my love for her in these words they lie.

No fancy gifts for her I can afford,
But would love to do so if I were a lord,
I would buy her all the gifts she would want,
And forget the bills that used to haunt.

But poor am I just of the common folk,
So for her these words are all I have wrote,
To get her to fall deeply in love,
With the writer of whom she always dreams of.

Street People

Have you ever sat alone in the dark?
Ever walked at night in an empty park?
It's a scary though to be all alone,
At this time of month with no one to phone.

But who are we to care, all comfy and nice,
Sitting at home with our heating and rice,
But pause for a moment and hold that thought,
Think of the ones who have less than nought.

Alone in the streets with no one to care,
No food on their plates cos no one will share,
What little they have is theirs to keep,
Some even without shoes upon their feet.

But at this time of year why should it matter,
When at least we all have food on our platter,
And at the end of the day when our meal is done,
Think of those people who are under the sun.

All of those people less fortunate than us,
For this time of year it's simply a must,
Warm clothes and shelter is all that they need,
Some food for their hunger even as small as a seed.

So just take a moment and hold onto that thought,
Before you sit down and eat all the food you just bought,
Perhaps go and look out in the streets,
And see if you can invite that person off the street.

Daybreak

The lights shine through the mist of the early morning,
The suns rays burst through the skinny branches of the trees,
Winters morn is icy and white,
As the sun glistens on the frozen lakes.

As we wake up to the beauty that surrounds us,
How often do we take time to look?
Nature has such wonders to offer,
Not in ancients lands or faraway places.

But look outside your very homes,
See the dawn of a new daybreak,
Everyday never the same,
Never a day where no colours exist.

So bright and vibrant the day's life begins,
The creatures stirring from their slumber,
Being awoken by the passing cars,
In the early hours of the dawn.

To watch the sun come up through the mist and fog,
And see the dew disperse from the heat of the day,
The life that sleeps now awakes,
To see this new and bright day break.

My Lady

From far away she speaks to me,
Her words that touch me deep inside,
I've not known this one for too much time,
But a heart she's stole one that's mine.

Her words she says may be false or true,
But there's something there and from then I knew,
That my love for her would forever grow,
Even though her name I do not know.

My thoughts of her are simply profane,
But they are all left in vain,
For I will never see her beauty inside,
Lost forever in the oceans tide.

A cover she keeps to protect her so,
Life's hurt she has learned but the pain still grows,
But forever in my heart she'll stay,
Till eternity and the end of day.

Love's Paradise

There was a time when all was calm,
No darkness around and no people to harm,
But what has happened, have we all gone mad,
Why have things turned out so bad?

I awake in the morning, another siren I hear,
Last nights shooting another dead body appears,
The insanity that surrounds us everyday,
Too much to bear, I need to get away.

I want to retreat to some faraway place,
Where no one runs and no one gives chase,
A place where I can find my own time,
Where no foul words are spoken but merely rhyme.

The poetic nature of one's heart will survive,
By peace and tranquillity it will be kept alive,
The freedom of thought will surround us all,
No one slaves of another man's soul.

And there your dreams will become so true,
With the hearts and mind of those you knew,
Who have joined you in this blissful place,
Forever by love an eternity embraced.

Death Wish

I can feel the sanity slipping away,
Within these walls confined to stay,
No windows or doors for me to escape,
Just these walls without a break.

My thoughts are trapped I cannot think,
I find myself falling, and beginning to sink,
Back to the depths where my past lays a waste,
Not given a thought, even in haste.

For the past is left forgotten, it's better that way,
Never to surface to see the light of day,
For it's the past that haunts me each and every day,
My mind it takes that keep slipping away.

For soon it will be my time to go,
And I look forward and welcome it so,
This nightmare I have that screws with my head,
Will no longer be here for I will be dead.

Nature's Blanket

As I wake up this morning and raise my weary head,
I look out of the window to see a world so dead,
A blanket of white that cuts through the dark sky,
I sit here and wait and watch time pass me by.

Such calm in the world when all's not awake,
Not a whisper of the animals that nature forsakes,
Just a pure white sheet that covers the world,
Waiting there for me, just to come and unfold.

The street lamps shine bright with an orangey glow,
I sit and watch the moonbeams dance so slow,
The cool breeze calling me to go outside,
But here I shall stay to bide my time.

The shadows lift as the sun appears across the night's sky,
Being chased away by the dawn flying high,
And the blanket of white that covers the ground,
Will slowly die without a whisper or sound.

And as I sit and through this window watch,
The dying beauty of natures love's lost,
And who knows when then next time I shall see,
Nature's blanket laid specially for me.

The Past Lurking

As I sit here in the silence,
My head pounding so clear,
For something lurks alone out there,
Something for all man to fear.

It knows not resistance,
For a futile effort it is,
And it knows no mercy,
So just give in to your fears.

It'll hunt you down wherever you are,
There is no place safe to hide,
There's little use in running,
For time is on its side.

So curious you are, as to what I speak,
Of this terror so profound,
It's in the mind of all of you,
For everywhere it can be found.

It stalks each and everyone,
Like a demon of the night,
It's your past that comes to haunt you,
So be sure to make it right.

Moonlight

Walking home on this cold frosty night,
I watch the moon as the Earth blocks it's light,
With an eerie glow it dies away,
Where is the light to pave my way?

The street lamps flicker as I walk past,
As if to say I will not last,
But why is that I say to myself,
"Forget it now it's just in your head".

I quicken my pace on this journey so long,
And sing to myself a life long song,
I remember the words I used to write,
In the cold and the lonely December nights.

Those words are what keep me going right now,
Through the cold, the wind and the icy snow,
I long for the comfort of my nice warm bed,
Instead of this walk of which brings me closer to death.

But finally I see that warm inviting glow,
Of my house that stands out through white of the snow,
And I think to myself of my long journey home,
And the thoughts that have crept into my mind so alone.

And as I approach the door to my house,
I stop and look back down the roads so close,
And at the moon that now begins to shine,
As if it to say that the night was mine.

Empty Space

I fell asleep late last night,
I dreamt that you were here, by my side,
But as I awoke and turned where you lay,
My smile disappeared, I saw the empty space.

Why did you have to leave me so soon?
My life has no meaning now that you've gone,
The sound of your voice lingers so long,
Like a ghost from the past that haunts my life's song.

So far away you are right now,
Across the waves of time,
Why did you have to leave?
My life now an empty rhyme.

But no matter how far apart we are,
Each other's hearts we share,
And no matter what life throws at me,
I'll always long for you to be there.

Mine

Why should I care what you do with you life?
When I am so happy here with my wife,
You were just some stranger to me,
So why do I have these feelings so deep.

Why should I care who you fuck every night?
It's not like you're mine to treat you so right,
Why do I care about the things that you do,
Why should I be jealous of him fucking with you?

Why do I feel all this hurting inside?
It cuts me so much like a ship through the tide,
I don't really know you from the next girl along,
So why all this jealousy inside me so strong?

The beds we both sleep in are not the one and same,
So why all these feelings, I know it sounds lame,
I can't get my mind from thoughts of you each day,
It gets so sad when you're the highlight of my day.

Some beautiful stranger I have no chance in hell,
That impacts my life when there's nothing to tell,
Oh fuck what the hell is wrong with me,
Why should I even let my heart bleed?

All the blood that comes out each cell crying in pain,
Who the fuck are you to make me feel this way?
My life was just fine when you weren't around,
And now look at this shit that's so profound.

Oh fuck this shit up I can't be bothered no more,
Why in the hell should I cry on the floor,
A stranger you are and will always be,
So why all the pain, what the fuck's wrong with me?

Sincere Words

Poetry and poems you don't seem to want,
Just pictures and words of my innermost thought,
To try to understand the person I am,
Don't even bother I am a complicated man.

All this stuff that I write, has inspiration at hand,
But does not truly reflect the man that I am?
The rhythm and rhyme that flows from my mind,
Are just stupid thoughts to bide my sweet time.

The kind of man that I hope to be,
Sincere and strong, every woman's dream,
Is just as shallow as the man inside,
For a woman's heart is all I desire.

But those that think they know who I am,
They don't know jack all they see is the tan,
They can' see past my shallow exterior,
There's a being inside more than the man in the mirror.

But am I really just fooling myself,
Is what everyone sees my real true self?
No past to hide and no regrets to run from,
Just living my life and every other Tom.

Am I really a person at peace with myself?
And there is no monster lurking in my head,
But what about the stuff that I write about,
Maybe it's not mine, just some other guys spout.

And these hands that type away on the keyboard so,
Are driven by this other one's force so low,
To write the words for you all to hear,
A man just bores you with his words so sincere.

Harmony

What in the world do you think about me?
Why are you so blind that you can't see?
How special I am for you to be,
Here with me for eternity.

You bitch and moan all day long,
After a hard days work I come home,
But you don't seem to appreciate me,
And the work I do for us to be free.

Why can't you see I do love you so,
But this love won't last the way you go,
I need some love back in return for me,
And not just demands that you want from me.

I thought you were different from all the rest,
I thought you'd appreciate my intellect,
The humour I have, you used to love so true,
And now it's just bad and I blame you.

For all the things we used to share,
Soon died down and made me aware,
That I need someone to appreciate me,
So that we could live in harmony.

Phone Call

I phone your home, but you're not there,
I phone your office and sit and stare,
No more numbers I have to call,
And now my life with no meaning at all.

I sit and wait for the phone to ring,
For that voice I know to make my heart sing,
But no phone call comes as I sit and wait,
Looking up at the clock I can see it's late.

I should learn to accept you don't want me near,
And now my heart so full of fear,
Of thoughts of rejection and things of that kind,
Are all that I can think of in my mind.

She Is...

She says she is blind,
But I want her to see,
She says she's a fool,
But she's so smart to me,
She says she's alone,
But I'm here for her to see.

Why can't she see my love's not blind?
How many times does she run through my mind?
All I want is for her to see,
That I'm always here for eternity.

She says that my love will lead her astray,
But who gives a damn if she's here to stay,
My life with no meaning until I saw that face,
But it's too late for now my mind I can't erase.

Why can't she see my love's not blind?
How many times does she run through my mind?
All I want is for her to see,
That I'm always here for eternity.

I used to say love was blind,
But who really believes in things of that kind,
Until I saw her face I thought so too,
But now all I want is to have her heart so true.

What is love if you're two worlds apart?
From the woman you love who thinks she's a tart,
She's always on my mind all day,
Why can't she see that I'd be hers to stay?

Why can't she see my love's not blind?
How many times does she run through my mind?
All I want is for her to see,
That I'm always here for eternity.

More Money

As I look up at the stars tonight,
I see your face through all the lights,
The streets are filled with empty words,
Just my mind and me are all that are heard.

I used to think that hope was true,
A worthless effort when I met you,
My heart it died on that very day,
To find your body where someone else lay.

What is the point in carrying on?
When your hope has been and gone,
This life so shallow, just as you,
More money is all that interested you,

The times we were together at last,
Just seemed to go by oh so fast,
And now that you have moved on,
Time just drags on and on.

What is the point in carrying on?
When your hope has been and gone,
This life so shallow, just as you,
More money is all that interested you.

But take advice from a broken man,
A woman whose heart can win a man,
Be careful what she says to you,
For money is all that they want from you.

What is the point in carrying on?
When your hope has been and gone,
This life so shallow, just as you,
More money is all that interested you.

What is the point in carrying on?
When your hope has been and gone,
This life so shallow, just as you,
More money is all that interested you.

Love's Apart

So many tears I cried,
All of those lonely nights,
My life with no meaning,
My heart with no feeling.

No sense do these words make,
Just pain for my life's sake,
Just empty words spoken,
And my soul all broken.

My life it had no meaning,
Until I found the feeling,
That burns within my heart,
For you even though we're apart.

Town

Why do I write these fucking words down?
When I know no one will read them in this damn town,
To escape from here is all we can do,
But where on this earth could we two go to.

This town is so dead, I need you now,
Come rescue this fool for I don't know how,
Hold me so tightly that my life will decease,
In your arms is where my resting place is.

What's there to be said in this song that I write,
It's full of the crap that I've not done with my life,
All my time I have wasted and youth left to die,
But all that's in vain if you're not by my side.

This town is so dead, I need you now,
Come rescue this fool for I don't know how,
Hold me so tightly that my life will decease,
In your arms is where my resting place is.

My life left to rot in this town that dies,
All of the bullshit they say and the lies,
I can't take any more of this life without you,
These words have no meaning unless you know they're for you.

This town is so dead, I need you now,
Come rescue this fool for I don't know how,
Hold me so tightly that my life will decease,
In your arms is where my resting place is.

Magic

Fairies do magic for some people to see,
You must be one to put this spell on me,
Through this forest of time you enchant me so,
My heart dances around, you make my soul glow.

You share your words with complete trust,
Your life like mine seems always a rush,
But when you're there time stands still,
You give my life meaning and something to will.

This magic that you used on me,
So beautiful just like your body to see,
It plays on my mind every forbidden night,
For my feelings just feel so right.

But are they cos of this spell on me,
I don't think that, that could ever be,
For these feelings for you so strong inside,
Could not be drowned by times precious tide.

Valentines Love

For you I write on this special day,
Of my love you brought my way,
Without you my life is never complete,
I thank the day when we first did meet.

And from that day we said "I do",
My heart has always thought of you,
These words are spoken from my heart,
My love for you could cut oceans apart.

And time and tide may come and go,
But my love for you will surely grow,
And I would like to say these words so few,
And they are that "I Love You".

Drugs Of War

These broken words lay on the floor,
Left there to rot like the scars of war,
Torn from affliction as the children once were,
Where is the terror that I used to incur?

The anger and hatred just burns in my veins,
All I have now is their blood on my brains,
The scars of the days when I used to rule high,
Now vanish like the drugs that lay by my side.

And that's all I know how to keep me alive,
Through these long lonely days and these cold winters nights,
I strike up a match, as I feel my lips sore,
I turn to my colleague who lies dead on the floor.

Is that what is left for me to do now,
Just keep lighting up until my life fades some how,
I remember the days when I was the rule,
But now they all laugh and call me a fool.

They know not the power I held in my hands,
These words that lay broken through times forgotten sands,
With a thunderous roar I could shoot them all dead,
And get under their skin and inside their heads.

But look at me now a crippled old fool,
Thinking of days since I had left school,
Just light up my last one to heal up these scars,
And make one last battle of my daily wars.

Brave Knight

As he enters the scene on his great white steed,
He sees his fair maiden imprisoned indeed,
With no fear of life just love in his hand,
He takes one the very lords of this land.

And as they fall down one by one,
He sees his fair maiden being held by some,
He draws on his bow and let's rip the cord,
Cuts them all down with his bare hands and sword.

And as the fair maiden falls down from the height,
He catches her fall and gazes at her sight,
For her beauty and love drove him here,
And now in his arms he can feel all the fear.

Of what it'd be like if she were not there,
In no need of rescuing from their hypnotizing stare,
But that would not happen for he'd always be there,
And no harm would come to her, not even her hair,

And off in the sunset these two would ride,
And make love so sweet through time's roaring tide,
A fairy tale princess and a brave knight together,
As I do one day wish it'd be like us in heaven.

Broken Words

Words broken
Silence spoken
Through ripping tides
Like you and I

Sweet love
Pouring rain
A good combination
For the insane

Gentle words
A Soft caress
Your body's warmth
On my bare chest

Utter nonsense
Or pure genius
You can decide
Whether I live or die

My Ecstasy

This may sound rude but I don't care,
I've got to tell you, I'm going spare,
I want to see your flesh on mine,
And be the one to touch you divine.

I want to feel your naked skin,
Please why won't you let me in,
The passion for you burns so strong,
If only you feel my heart's long.

I need to feel me inside of you,
I pray that one day this dream will come true,
And until then I'll imagine us so,
In ecstasy forever our bodies moving so slow.

These words are foul but from my heart,
I hope that these words are just the start,
For one day if we ever meet,
These words will be true, and your love so sweet.

Death's Eternity

With that gun to your head,
You shoot my heart dead,
And the soul that will rise,
Will be yours in my eyes.

Then death will wait,
For you by the gates,
And my name will ring proud,
As that trigger sounds loud.

Then join me you will,
In the night's air so still,
And together we will be,
Immortal for eternity.

Unspoken Words

I've got something to tell you, I've got something to say.
My feelings for you deep inside, they cannot go away,
You're in my head constantly, I just cannot be without,
The thought of you so far away, it kills my bleeding heart.

You know how much I love you, with everything inside,
I can't describe the pain I feel without you by my side,
And yes I have a life to lead, a family of my own,
But I'll never forget you, you're engraved within my bones.

I know I shouldn't feel this way, it just seems so very wrong,
But how can I ignore it, when my feelings are this strong,
I know I'll survive with this feeling, but I know it will take time,
For now I have you as a friend, I know you can't be mine.

I just want you to know how crazy, my head just spins inside,
I wish I could explain to you, with words that aren't so blind,
I want to shout out how I feel and scream it to the world,
If only it was that simple, I'd stand by and watch it explode.

I don't know how you read these words, I cannot see your face,
I wonder if there's a tear there, maybe hidden deep in place,
I don't know how you feel inside, and I know I never will,
Some words are best unspoken, but know I love you still.

Inside Man

Look at me, tell me, what do you see?
Do you see the man inside, or just the outside me?
Cos the man inside is dying, and for them it doesn't show,
But I know you can see through it, you have seen it grow,

I once had a life like yours, full of happiness and joy,
Only to see it disappear, broken like a toy,
I want to gain my life back, but it seems I don't know how,
And that is when you walked in, and hoped you'd show me somehow.

You gave my life some meaning, some purpose to it all,
Those happy days I once had, to return to me once more,
And when you stood right by my side, the memories haunt me still,
I felt your warmth and gentle heart, and then I had the will.

You showed me how to love again, and to remind me what I missed,
You helped me through a strange old time, and sealed it with a kiss,
Forever locked into my head, from now until I die,
You helped me find myself again, you resurrected the man inside.

And now I begin my journey, back to help the man inside,
The one that you helped to save, the one that almost died,
But they don't still understand, or even know the truth,
How close I was to breaking, if it wasn't just for you.

Little Vikki

I got down on my knees for her, because she is so short,
A little girl that I know, she wore a short skirt,
A gentle little creature, with passion in her eyes,
Her name is little Vikki and she gave me a surprise.

Such caring and compassion, she made tea for me each day,
And everyday she'd smile at me; I felt I have to say,
I thank her for her every move and laughs she used to share,
And especially I love the way she had her dark hair.

So this I write, an ode to her, just because I need to say,
No matter where I felt I should be, I knew she'll lead the way,
But now I have to leave her, and all the rest behind,
So these words are for Little Vikki, because she stole my mind.

Souls Pain

Confusion, Lies, Deception is that what my life is now?
Trying to find the meaning, in these words that I write down,
What the hell am I doing, how do I make it stop,
I want to get back to me, and things I have forgot,

So here I write whatever I think, and hope it goes away
Written in ink and out of my head, to be found another day,
I don't know what I'm doing, everything is blurred
I want to be normal, does that sound so absurd?

I need to find something again, without the pain or hurt,
How can I be happy with all this on my heart?
I know why people go crazy, and why they go insane,
Because the life and soul of theirs is replaced with only pain.

Kiss Started

I still feel so much inside I wish I could let you know,
A schoolboy with a crush perhaps, but what can I do?
I know I can't give you much, except my heart and soul,
But I've done that already, others can see it so,
I don't know what I should do or how to continue my life,
I have a child, I have a home, and a very loving wife,
Maybe I should tell her my heart has now been shared,
I can't think now, I'm so confused, why should I even care,
Do I continue living, my life with all these lies?
Or should I reveal my inner truths that lie behind these eyes,
For once my life is so confused, I can't recover from this,
And all because something changed, that started with a kiss.

BRNO

I visited a city not so far away,
A city filled with wonder, in every single way,
My heart and soul it captured, never to return,
Without a word of warning, the emptiness now burns,

I can't describe the way I feel, for this city so far,
And the loneliness and sadness that deep fills my heart,
Can someone please help me, my head it hurts so much,
I can't stand to be away, so far away from touch.

I wonder when I might see the beloved city again,
The one that I have wrote about, and suffer all this pain,
So whosoever reads this, I'll tell you of where I speak,
A city known as Brno, that I forever long to meet.

You Are…

Inside my heart is dying,
Can't the world see…?
There's nothing left inside me,
Nothing more for me to give,
My tears dried up,
No feelings left,
My blood has turn to wine,
And no one can see me,
Inside my heart has died,

You are my inspiration,
You are my joy,
You are my motivation,
You are my toy,
You are my weakness,
You are my pain,
You are my strengths,
You are my everything.

Real Love

Like a distant star she shines so bright,
Someone there to light up the night,
In those darkest moments when all seems lost,
She's there for me, when I need her the most,
I hope she knows just how I feel,
Sometimes I can hardly believe how real,
My love for her inside it grows,
I just have to tell her, so she knows….

Times Grace

I just want to sit here in silence and solitude,
I just want you to know, that you are my fortitude,
As time graces us with each passing moment,
I long to see you again... if only for a second.
I know how time can never take us back,
We can't live in the past, of one moment we enjoyed,
But in my head are thoughts of you that linger to this day,
I wish somehow it wouldn't hurt as much with you so far away,
They say that time's a healer, but what if I don't want to be healed?
If healing means my thoughts of you, will somehow disappear,
I'd rather grow old and grey with this pain inside my heart,
And knowing that somewhere in life, I touched another's past.
Yes it's you I'm really talking about.. you I really miss.
And I hope these words I write will remind you of that long and distant kiss..

Hooked

Life's twist of fate brought you to me,
Never for once did I know how I could feel this way,
Torn between right and wrong,
Love brought you to me and for now it's gone,
I can't describe the way I feel,
Only know that my love for you is truly real,
Not just empty words thrown in the air,
When I say I love you, I really care,
Tears stroll down my cheek with thoughts of you,
The times we shared, even though they were few,
I miss you... can't you tell?
You've got my hooked, under your spell...

Orphan Child

Picture me, sitting here.. all alone in the world,
A little boy stretching out his hand, for someone to hold,
They walk right past me, with not a tear in there eyes,
Can't they show some compassion, for this lonely orphan child.

It seems like hope and faith caught the last train out tonight,
And all that's left is misery and despair of that orphan child,
Please oh god help them all, give them someone for they may see,
What they neglect when they walk down these old London streets..

As the weather turns colder, and the nights are drawing in,
These streets I wander desperately, but find nothing there but sin,
Can no one see this orphan child, struggling all alone,
It's time that someone see's it all and offers him a home.

it seems like hope and faith caught the last train out tonight,
And all that's left is misery and despair of that orphan child,
Please oh god help them all, give them someone for they may see,
What they neglect when they walk down these old London streets..

That place to offer shelter, some comfort and warmth,
A place where they can go to, to catch the train of hope,
A world outside our own front door, that is no longer blind,
And now the world of the orphan child, a world filled with light.

Goodbyes

Don't tell me what I can't do... as I've been further than you know,
You think you have your own issues... well baby I've got to go,
Thanks for all the times we shared .. but honey you ain't the one,
Time to move on, time to grow, cos it's been a while since I learnt.

Gold digging just ain't my style you should have known that from the start,
So why the hell you played on me and kept messing with my heart,
I'm all grown up and see right through all the lies you put me through,
When creeping to your mans house.. girl I'm glad we're through.

You should have learned to keep your cool, and stopped messing round my back,
You thought I wouldn't notice.. well baby he can have you back,
You can take the money and the cars cos baby you ain't worth my time,
But after all is said and done, what's worse now you're not mine.

Go ahead and pack your bags. and leave the keys upon the side,
Just turn your back and no goodbye's cos I sure ain't gonna cry,
And don't for one sec turn around and think you're gonna see me die,
Cos baby I'm stronger than you know, and you know that ain't no lie.

Something Beautiful

I want to write something beautiful, especially for you,
I want you to know how special you are, and know these words are true,
Sometimes I feel I've lost myself, with my thoughts and ideas of you,
I don't know how to express how I feel, and so these words I write so new.

I know that I've been crazy, done some silly things in the past,
I guess I'm just human, trying to make something last,
I found it so hard to tell you, all the things on my mind,
Now I fear I'm loosing you, and whatever was inside.

Please don't say you hate me, or feel guilty for my pain,
Just tell me that you love me, and everything is still the same,
I know that life changes and we cannot see what's next,
I never expected to be writing these words, or sending you a text.

Today I'm opening up myself, for you to see me in truth,,
No misleading words, or secret thoughts, nothing kept from you no more,
I still find it hard to open up, so please be patient and give me time,
I've never had a friend like you, or a lover in my mind.

And so I'm thankful that you came, wandering into my life,
Please don't be sad that I never told you she was my wife,
It's all my fault I hope you see, how hard this hurts for me inside,
I love you more than you know, just like the oceans flowing tide.

Far Away City

A city so far away from here,
Leaves me speechless, like nobody knows,
I sit here thinking of what has past,
A dream come true, but could it last.

Nights like dreams, come and go so fast,
Days so pure, what more could I ask,
But something just so alien about it all,
Something in my mind I can't describe.

Tell me how I can sit here now,
And think of everything I know somehow,
This dream has come to an end,
And then back to my life it will truly be.

Something's were always on my mind,
But now they just sit here and fade and die,
What things can possibly pass in my mind,
Am I dreaming? Or am I alive !!!

Thinking

Do you still think about me, the way I do for you?
It's been a while now, I thought time would heal,
I don't regret the things we did, or the time we shared together,
I do believe it was destiny that changed our lives forever.

I wonder if you really, still think of me at all?
I wish time has been kinder on you, then it has on me,
I can't believe I feel this way just feeling so torn apart,
What was I thinking, giving you my only heart.

I don't regret a single moment I spent while you were here,
I hope that the same goes for you, no matter where you are,
If you were here face to face, the things I'd share with you,
To look, feel and hear things, from my point of view

I know some people say, "if things were different",
But that is not something I would say,
If things in my life never happened, I know won't feel the pain,
Of never knowing someone like you, someone to help me through the rain.

Pretend

Why do we lie to ourselves?
Pretend to be someone else,
I know who I am but am I fooling myself?
Could a person like me, ever change?

Years from now will I look back and say,
Nothing about me has ever changed,
Do you think years from now I'll be the same?
Or can I stand up and make that change?

I've lied to myself, one too many times,
Lost myself in too many rhymes,
And every day I wake not feeling complete,
Do I lie to myself, until my maker I meet?

Am I meant for something more than this?
Something bigger, so I prove I exist,
Am I started to discover who I am,
Or faces in the crowd like any man?

Heroes

In a world with no heroes, where do I stand?
A boy with no future, and no past in his hands,
I sit here and wonder is this all life can be ,
With nothing left in store in this world for me.

I know that I'm different, Somehow not the same,
I feel that I might be going insane,
Can someone please tell me is this all I am?
A boy with no future, and no past in his hands.

Am I not the hero that I think I am?
Just a foolish man dreams, with no purpose or plan,
No soul to be saved, no life to protect,
A heroes dream dies, with no cause or effect.

Is this really the man that I think I am?
A man with no life and no past in my hands,
Or am I just scared of what might become?
If I pull the trigger of this loaded gun!!!

Hearts World Apart

Do you know what you've done to me?
When did you realise all I can be?
I saw that look in your eyes, the very first day,
How long did it take you to feel that way?
We both should've known it could never be,
No matter how bad we want it, one of life's miseries.
And now we both stand, two worlds apart.
Thinking of what we've done to our hearts,
Some things in life weren't meant to be,
Like me and you one of life's tragedies,
Maybe one day we shall meet again?
Another place, another time to go through the pain,
I'm sure in this play, our secrets our kept,
There's no way I believe that this is for nought,
In life's plans for me, there things left to be sought,
I can't believe that this is the end,
When I know in my head that my heart needs to mend,
I can say with conviction my plans are not done,
So with these words I end, my life just began

Undiscovered

Have you ever felt like there is something more?
Something missing but you're just not sure,
You can feel it in your soul,
You just feel un-whole,
On the verge of something new,
But you still don't have a clue,
Tell me what you feel right now?
Agree with me, or just say no,
My purpose in life is still to be seen,
But I know I'm meant for greater things,
Or am I just deluding myself,
Into believing I'm not the man I am,
Denying all that is brought to me to deal,
Looking back on my life, is it all real?
Tell me what you're thinking?
Through these words so tangled up,
Maybe you can find the answers,
That are eluding me.

Reminiscent Thoughts

It still hurts for me I try so hard,
I thought with this time I'd forgot,
The pain still hurts I can't explain why,
I still miss you when you're, not in my life.

I can't believe why I feel this way,
Have you put a spell on me?
Do you feel the same way still?
Does it hurt?

There's not a day goes by I'm not reminded of you,
I know we didn't plan this,
It hurts that I can't express how I feel,
I know the pain it would cause.

It's funny how life turns out,
Seems like the pages of a book,
Telling a story with each passing word,
But the book is still unfinished,
I wonder if there'll be another chapter with you,
I know for now it can never be true,
But an unfinished book still needs to end,
I'm glad I'm the one with the pen in my hand.

No Regrets

No regrets, is what I say,
I can't help but feel this way,
The pain has become a part of my life,
Hidden deep within, far from my wife,
The outside so cool and so calm,
Told only by my sweaty palm,
Distant memories locked away,
Never to see the light of day,
Far from it all, out of sight,
I keep the pain in the deep of the night,
I woke up quickly in the darkness still,
Dreaming of you on the window sill,
Far, far away here no one knows,
How I feel of life's deep woes,
I never could imagine that one day,
I'd feel the pain forever this way.

Ink's Run

Write down my thoughts on a bit of paper,
See where the pen takes me,
Thinking of her as I always do,
Should I? Would I? Could I?
Let the ink run on the plain blank page,
Flowing like the oceans waves,
My thoughts they wonder to and fro,
Sitting here thinking about the past,
How my life has taken me.
How my work has consumed me.
Times where I have lost myself.
Only to become stronger, smarter, experienced.
Choices were made whether good or bad.
Still more to come, who knows?
In the design of my life, a plan or map.
Still I continue my journey to better understand myself.
I don't think I've found or been all I can be,
I want to be much more than me,
Leave something behind to say I was here,
Not to be forgotten in time and rhyme.
I'm sure now I feel stronger than ever,
About my life, who I am, now and forever,
For I am myself, not fully discovered,
Just ink and a pen for the words to uncover.

Thoughts

You know I cannot cry,
So why do I still try?
My emotions plain to see,
Just what you've done to me,
Lonely since you've left now,
Got to get my life back somehow,
Been missing you since you've gone,
How can this be so wrong?
Did you know how you'd enter my life?
Cut me deep just like a knife,
Then leave the wound for all to see,
Another of life's miseries.

Love's Loss

Time's love lost with nothing to fear,
Trapped in memories, not so near,
Though time is jaded by my life,
Who knew it would cut like a knife,
Leave me alone with my words so pure,
Left with time, for them to cure,
I ask nothing no more for it's far too late,
Maybe your soul and mine were meant to mate,
Forget what path you've been led upon,
For mine has been torn apart so long,
I can't remember the times gone by,
When I had a life without a lie,
God, please forgive me for all my sins,
Without them written, I can't begin,
And life is now one big blur,
Please save me, save me from her.

Poisoned Words

Do you know what you've done to me?
It still hurts so much,
Inside it burns so fierce and strong,
How much longer can I hold on?

I need to forget about you, I don't know how!
Your poisoned words engraved somehow,
I don't know why, I feel like this,
But without you I can't exist.

Can't you see I'm dying inside?
Without you I have no purpose in life,
Please tell me what I need to do,
Because right now all I want is you.

Please forgive me for all my sins,
I can't believe what life brings,
Who knew that I would end up this way,
Lost and confused throughout the day.

Look at what you have done to me!
It's there in my face, it's plain to see,
This charade I know I can't sustain,
And hopefully I'll no longer feel the pain.

Promises Changed

You said to me you loved me,
Was it a lie?

You said to me you'll save me,
Emptiness fills my heart.

You said you'll forever remember me,
Now forgotten by times cruel fate.

I said I'd never leave you,
Yet here I am so far.

I said to you I'll protect you,
But I can't find the faith.

I said you'll forever be mine,
Only now to be torn apart.

You said you'll forever love me,
I said I'll always love you.

What's changed!!!

Words Moan

Get out of my head, leave me alone,
It's my own words to allow me to moan,
Tear my heart as you've done before,
Leave me this way on love's sweet door,
Cut my soul and leave it to dry,
Hung out, left like a butterfly,
Call me names and walk out of my life,
Leave me this sorrow that cuts like a knife.
Kill me from inside; it's what you do best,
Maybe this is one of life's little tests,
Who knows if I'll survive it, but I do know this,
You walked out on me, as you should,
In time I'll heal my open wounds,
Just as yours have healed, a little too soon,
You left me one of life's deepest experience,
And now you're gone I'm left behind,
Soon to join you in a little time.

Nights Death

The fire was high on that darkened eve,
As the nights air made it hard to breathe,
I struggled home on these dimly lit streets,
Hastening not to greet the man next to me,
As the time goes by on my journey's long,
I whistle a line or sing out a song,
For soon I shall arrive at my place at home,
For death shall soon consume my soul.

Freeze

Freeze Frame, all insane,
Come to me and free your pain,
Hold up, what's here,
Shoot me now or face the fear,
Wake up, go to town,
Kill a guy, going down,
Doing time, hang five,
Shallow hearts, big words,
What in life to live or die,
Sounding to me like a sheep in the herd,
Rain, rain, go away,
Never come again today,
Forest fires all put out,
By my pains incessant spout,

Leaving Sun

As they leave one by one,
To their homes with open arms,
I sit here and chat to thee,
And wonder how ironic life can be.

The sun's rays creep so slow,
To tempt me home to the people I know,
To sit outside and cut the grass,
And think of times that have long been past.

Sin's Tears

These tears I cry for you,
Come save my soul my love,
Blood falling from my eyes so true,
Under this moons darkened glove.

These tears burn my heart,
And rip out my life's soul,
Do you think we could restart?
What love made us whole?

Drowning in the blood of my tears,
Someone come save me,
Please come and erase all my fears,
I've fallen on my knees.

What heaven would take me in,
Murdered by loves death begun,
Lived in a world full of lies and sin,
Come and undo what you have done.

Loves Lost Mind

It's been a long time now,
I still feel the pain,
Summer's ended somehow,
I'm left with the rain.

Is it the same for you?
Bleeding deep inside,
Do you feel me too?
Heartache every night.

I can't kill this feeling,
I wanted you to know,
My heart, it's just not healing,
But this it cannot show.

I wish I could tell you,
How I feel inside,
I'm scared if you only knew,
You'd also loose your mind.

Man

How different a creature, man?
How noble in his efforts,
How confident in his desires,
What is a man, if not to live?

Unique in his identity,
Created out of purpose,
Someone to have compassion upon,
Seldom do we think of man,
The uniqueness he possesses,
Free is man in his thoughts,
Powerful is he in dreams,
Deadly in his imagination.

The highest of creation,
But what is man's price,
Through man's triumphs, blood,
Man's wars torn apart,
His imagination black as coal,
Or white as the purest snow,
Man? Ignited by greed and wealth,
Or driven by purity and love?
Man, how different a creature?

Old House

Tiredness creeps in for the night,
I sit back and relax under this light,
The wind howls at my window's pane,
And the falling down of the incessant rain,
All stir up feelings best left to rot,
Like an old army wound best left forgot,
My pipe lays aside with it's ember dying away,
As if to say it'll be you someday.

I stoke the fire and watch it grow,
Flames dancing around my mortal soul,
Seemingly they all laugh at me,
Dying away with smiles of glee,
As if to say your time is soon,
Just as the sun chases the moon,
And so I sit back in this old oak chair,
Just to look in the mirror at my white hair.

This old house is all I have left in the end,
This pipe by my side my only friend,
And the clock on the wall that ticks away,
With each passing moment my life fading away.

Lost Words

A lonely bruised sheep,
Then a gun to my head,
A bullet in hand,
And a dead man's band,
A superficial tale,
Told not so long ago,
My love for you being sold no more,
The tales of rhyme,
That wash ashore,
That hanging noose,
To hang no more,
A lovers tear,
With no regret,
An angels heart,
Now burnt with death,
The endless nights,
That run no more,
Wounded soldiers,
Line the floors,
A broken down man,
With no love to be found,
That gun to his head,
Now in his blood he is drowned.

Future's Past

Tell me about the things of the past?
How did you seem to make it all last,
When time stood still for you and I,
Unified in the blink of an eye.

Where a dreamers dream can tell no lie,
And the futures past in the blink of an eye,
Where rain falls down to a beating drum,
To raise the dead of kingdom come.

Once more the armies lay in wait,
The past and future both await,
A war ahead to end all wars,
The time is now to settle the scores.

The futures set, but not in stone,
A man's castle is his home,
And from then his fate and destiny,
forever his own to eternity.

Dance the Night Away

Just as sure as the stars burn bright in the sky,
The world keeps turning like you and I,
And even though the darkness will prevail,
It's you and me that will live the tale.

For now it's time to say goodbye,
To all those things we used to like,
And forever things will go astray,
But for you and me we'll dance the night away.

Just keep the sun from chasing the moon,
Like you and I we'll too fade soon,
In times bitter sweet eternity,
Lost in this worlds congeniality.

Through these hard times and through it all,
We'll see each other's mortal souls,
And bear the lives of a thousand screams,
To dance this dance and live our dreams.

For now it's time to say goodbye,
To all those things we used to like,
And forever things will go astray,
But for you and me we'll dance the night away.

Souls Eternity

Like a bullet to your brain,
Driving you insane,
Falling to your knees,
Your heart openly bleeds,

Burning at your soul,
For you there is no more,
Extinguishing the flame,
You once sought to gain,

Trapped inside your head,
Wishing you were dead,
Cutting like a knife,
Fall your ending life,

Freedom of your soul,
Eternity unfolds,
Soon you will be mine,
Forever sealed in time.

Inside War

Can you feel it brewing deep down inside,
A war to shape the future,
Coming with the tides,
You know that it's about to start,
But you cannot tell when,
You know that it is close though,
And your time is gonna end.
You've seen it in the darkness,
Searched within your soul,
Ever dying embers,
With nothing or no goal,
You should have learned to stop it
When you were just a boy,
But something told you not to,
And let it burn with joy.
You know the war so well now,
It's haunted all your dreams,
With a burden only you should know,
It's strange, or so it seems,
You know that it's about to begin,
Because you will let go,
And all the rage and passion,
Will kindly let you go,
Unleash it all inside yourself,
For it's the only way,
To save them from this war,
Inside you, burning away.

Distant Family

And so here I sit again, waiting to depart,
Back to the city where I once was, the one that stole my heart,
Now to face the thoughts again, if ever I shall return,
Left with haunting memories, Left in time to burn,
I hope that when you read this, you will come to know,
The feelings that I feel right now, the ones that fill me so,
Of laughter and compassion, for a family that I know,
To have to leave them all behind, is the hardest thing I do,
To some friends that are leaving, I dedicate these words,
Some things said to remember, some may sound absurd,
So please don't think that I forget, you're forever in my heart,
I remember everything, we were together from the start,
I wish you all the best in life, and all the joy and love you seek,
And if you're ever feeling down, remember one day we'll meet.
And reminisce about the times, we shared throughout our lives,
And how we came together, forever our lives entwined,
So please remember all my words, and especially myself,
Because I write them all for you, with whom I'd be no help,
And always remember that one day, we'll all meet again,
Till then you stay inside my heart, to help me through the rain.

Frozen Reaper

The futures always changing,
Time's reaper upon the chase,
Freeze this moment, keep it!
So never to erase.

If only it were possible,
Times dealer laid to rest,
Live forever in the moment,
The rest is just a test.

Life's dream to be reality,
Forever, held in time,
Save me from time's suicide,
And heal my hearts lost rhyme,

Look to me for saviour,
For I feel I am no more,
Without these precious moments,
Do I want to love no more?

Over Again

I thought I was over it!
I thought it had gone!
And now I return back again,
These feelings are reborn.

And so again I hide,
How I really feel inside,
Go back to being "me" again,
Finding words to keep me alive.

I'm sure that people know,
Can't they tell it from my face?
This man may hide his thoughts,
But the body doesn't lie.

It knows just how the pain feels,
And reveals for all to see,
If they really understand,
For them it's plain to see.

So I'm being "me" again,
Although it is the same,
I can't pretend it isn't,
Because some things never change.

I Want...

I want to write down words for you,
I want to bleed inside,
I want to cure this hurt I feel,
I want to feel alive,
I want you to not ignore me,
I want you to say it's true,
I want you to keep believing,
I want to know you do.
I want you not to forget me
I want to hear it from inside
I want to hear your voice again,
I want you in my life
I know I can't write to you,
I know I do not bleed,
I know I can't cure the hurt I feel,
I know I am alive,
I know you don't ignore me,
I know you say it's true,
I know you'll keep believing,
I know that inside you do,
I know you won't forget me,
I know you hear it too,
I know I'll hear your voice again,
I know you're in my life.

Leaving

You told me you were leaving,
I had to say goodbye,
A new chapter in your book of life,
It's amazing how time flies,

I don't know how to tell you,
You mean the world to me,
A friend and special colleague,
You're just like my family.

And so I hope you'll stay in touch,
I know you'll be just fine,
Because time can heal many things
It'll heal your heart and mine.

So take care my little angel,
I bid you farewell for now,
I'll see you in the future,
I'll find a way somehow.

Live free ..

Live to be free,
Live for your dreams,
Live like there's no tomorrow to be seen.

Live as yourself,
Live to die,
Live like you're always so fucking high.

Live for the here,
Live for the now,
Live to make yourself feel proud.

Live to regret,
Live to be burnt,
Live like you never want her to hurt.

Live for the fire,
Live for the ice,
Live for your soul and never think twice.

Live to be seen,
Live to survive,
Live your life, like there's nothing to hide.

Live in your world,
Live in mine,
Live with me together for all time.

Realisation

Waking up, a new dawn appears,
A realisation, now becomes clear,
This life of mine, a map ahead,
Played out for me, until I am dead.

My decisions my own but destined to be,
My life already written out for me,
My choices I make may all pre-planed,
By a force unknown, but greater than man.

The choices I've made all been my own,
Realising now that they've all been known,
Regret and forgiveness now go hand-in-hand,
For things I have done have all been planned.

Orchestrated my world and all things around,
It's only now that I've been found,
And what I do the choices I've made,
Written in history, where they've now been played.

So the future for me is all so clear,
I don't have regrets, and no real fear,
For whatever life holds, in store for me,
I know that any other just can never be.

Just as the people I've met in my life,
The day I decided to marry my wife,
All part of bigger plans written for me,
True to life, my fate, my loves and true destiny.

I understand now, how I fit right in,
The grand scheme of things, where I have been,
Just a pawn in this play, playing my part,
Realising this, my life's about to start.

Wings

Walking softly through fields no more,
Voices speaking, my head so sore,
Someone please listen, I am falling,
Pick up the pieces of my life,
Slowly, heart reviving,
Can you bring me life?
Soul's immortal longing,
Searching to belong,
Is there no one out there?
Catch my fall from grace,
Sometimes death so longing,
Feel my own disgrace,
Can you still not hear me?
Maybe I'm too quiet,
Please hear my forgiveness,
In the darkest of the night,
Tell me that you love me,
Heal my scars with blood,
Give my life salvation,
Lifting my soul high up,
When did my wings fall?
I feel it all so cold,
Someone find them fallen,
Revive my mortal soul.

Heaven's Door

Time's war

Souls no more

Trapped inside

A fading life

Looking down

Worlds drowned

Consumed flame

Driving me insane

Unlock the door

Give me the key

Steal my heart

Set me free

Angels breath

Blow into me

Take me to heaven

Let me be

Rain

As the rain falls, bouncing off the floor,
Standing, tears bleeding from my eyes,
She turns and walks away,
Running out my life.

Left alone with nature's comfort,
Could it be, I seek my own worth,
Memories like drops, fall out of my mind,
Echoes of the past, poisoned by time.

Splashing drops now soaking me through,
This morning's weather seems now overdue,
Was it what I need to wake me from sleep,
Stirring inside, something so deep.

Nature's consummation of my own self,
My souls abduction, needing no help,
I stand here now enjoying the rain,
With each passing drop, taking my pain.

Don't Look Back

I can see the sunlight fading,
I see it in your eyes,
Don't tell me you're heart is dying,
I hear it in your mind,
Come to me for the last time baby,
I just wanted you to know,
No matter what life's dealing,
I think it's time to let go.

Let me go this very moment,
And let us never look back,
We've had our fun my darling,
All our secrets kept,
But don't look back my baby,
Cos I'm feeling no regrets,
It's time we move on honey,
So don't look back.

Remember all the time's we shared,
Forget about all the pain,
Think about how good we had it,
And know you're not the one to blame,
Time has shown our paths now ending,
We've both had our fun,
So don't look back my baby,
Our lives have just begun.

My Last Breath

I try to sit here and forget,
My mind filled with sorrow and regret,
Two worlds seemingly collide,
Lost in a sinful deadly mind,

The war has been fought and lost,
Minds taken over by lust,
Poison slipping in your eyes,
Becoming blind to my disguise,

The silence quiet yet so loud,
Deafened by thoughts in a crowd,
Can you not hear me fall down?
Slowly seeping in the ground.

Can you not hear my voice?
Too late or no more choice?
Is it time to let go and accept?
That maybe now is my death.

No more trying to forget,
No wars left in my head,
The silence soon to be unheard,
My last breaths are for her…

Memories Words

I have no idea what to tell her,
It seems no words to say,
No words to do my heart justice,
So I let them slip away,

One day I know I'll say them,
But for now they're locked away,
Stolen in my memories,
For now that's where they'll stay,

When I'm old I'll tell her,
All the things I want to say,
I'll stand upon the precipice,
I'll blow them all away,

So finally she'll hear them,
No longer locked away,
Brought forth from my memories,
For her they'll always stay.

Heavens Fall

These hearts, no longer are ours,
Torn from us, like worlds apart,
Capture my soul and set it free,
Leave this world and let me be,

Above the heavens, you descend,
Feel my love, can you comprehend?
Love's fire, it burns so bright,
Lifting me up into your light.

You capture my body and my soul,
Without you, my life's not whole,
Split between heaven and hell,
Into your arms I slowly fell,

Let me share my soul with you,
Put back together, a different view,
Let me show you love's burning desire,
At last our hearts saved from the fire.

Souls Entombment

Souls death, bleeding no more,
The hurt of it all, no longer sore,
Passions heart burned to the ground,
Love's saviour, nowhere to be found.

Die for the love, your soul to be saved,
No longer entombed, your mind now enslaved,
Talk to me, save me, I need you to know,
Death's only the start, so where did you go?

Love's eternity dying, forever be burned,
Screaming so loud, it's silence unheard,
Find me again, like you did me before,
Come save my soul, let it burn me no more.

Caught between lust and the sins of the past,
Knowing these words were not meant to last,
Heal my souls bleeding, take it away,
Come to me baby, forever we'll stay.

Leave Me Alone

Why do they think I can cope with it all?
In adversity's face I can't save no more,
My life just a slave to the helping of man,
Can they not see I've done, all that I can?

Helping them all, are they blind, can't they see?
Killing my soul, until deaths eternity,
Falling from grace, one by one do they know?
Pieces of life just burn from my soul.

One day I'll awake and it'll all be a dream,
Some fucked up nightmare, with no one to be seen,
And slowly I'll lie in my grave to be freed,
Hoping and praying my love will come save me.

No one will care what I've done in this world,
No mark for this man, only whispers unheard,
So still I am here just to make my own way,
Leave something behind, to show that I stayed.

Trying to change the world by just being me,
Leave me alone, so one day I'll be free,
Can they not figure, that they have it in them,
Potential to grow, beyond any man,
Use the power of life, as a map or a plan,
A guide for them all, wherever they may be.,
Just leave me alone, and let your conscience be free.

Love's War

Suicide's love took away all I feel,
Cut me down, so that I can heal,
Poisoned by love's darkest defeat,
Into my eyes, you feel the deceit.

Destined to lie across life's tomb,
Resurrected around earths doom,
A kiss destroying sanity's mind,
Take another life, for mine in kind.

Together we face destruction alone,
Divided by loves heart, so unknown,
Guide me to light, like I felt before,
Rip my heart out, let's start love's war.

Stood across love's battlefield earth,
Can you feel your own hearts' worth?
Kept alive by the scorching of time,
Together we rule this kingdom of mine.

Let me fall, to death's eternal peace,
Kept souls alive but out of reach,
We'll be united after this war,
Left with a heart still longing for more.

Stolen Moments

Stolen moments we try to forget,
Time's lost soul, eternities regret,
Forget me now, how I used to be,
Live my life, set yourself free,

Capture my soul and bleed it dry,
Leave me alone, within your mind's eye,
Consume my heart, with your soul of desire,
Steal me away from hells burning fire,

Take me away and let it all go,
Help me to live through another's lost soul,
Watch myself fall, through the endless time,
Sleeping forever, your soul in mine.

Hollow Tomb

You said to me you'd be here, I wanted it so,
Carved out of my heart, your immortal soul,
Stuck between life and loves forever doom,
Cast me aside to your never ending tomb.

Slowly to sink to oblivions death,
Light fading fast, no more regrets,
Forbidden sin, was all that I was,
Now left to rot, inside these four walls.

Memories fading through a distant facade,
Trapped by my sins, of that in the past,
Redemption for me no longer allowed,
Stolen by time, a nightmare so loud,

Drowning in darkness, the light fades away,
No longer to see another bright day,
Finally resting, my sins to be gone,
Leaving my heart, to Earth's hollow ground.

Confined Soul

Tears fill my eyes, hearts bleeding desire,
Stop myself falling, hearts feeling the fire,
Burst out of life, to a new worlds surround,
Lift me beyond, this souls suffering mound.

Still in the calmness, I hear it so loud,
Killing my head, like a lost ones child,
Pour out my soul, let me bleed it all out,
Leave nothing of me, just scream and then shout.

Feel my insides; let me show you my soul,
Condemned to this life, no longer so whole,
Writhing inside agony's hate and deceit,
Shelter myself from evils loathing defeat.

Close my senses, hide me away,
Help me to feel, no longer this way,
One day you'll save me, no longer confined,
Come save me my love, come find me alive.

Begging Hearts

Why do we put our hearts through this?
When we know all the pain that we miss,
Again to the brink of deaths open door,
Come to me again, to settle the score.

For a taste of heaven we go through hell,
Locked in our lives, by loves suicide shell,
Torn apart from loves cruel hand,
Twisted by life's uncompromising demands.

Join me in a song to take the pain away,
Reach for my arms and beg me to stay,
I cannot go through all the torture again,
When will this ceaseless pain seem to end?

Drowning in loves unmerciful tears,
Passion and desire, beginning to fear,
Feeling deaths knock on the door,
I cut out my heart and still beg for more.

Tears

You don't need to cry no more,
Precious tears, your eyes turn sore,
Let me kiss your lips and heal,
Stop your crying, I know how you feel.

Those tears burn just as much on me,
I feel the drops, they hurt and sting,
Use my shoulder to lift you up,
Stop your crying, I'll pick you up.

You know we both feel the same,
Though far apart, through this rain,
Your tears, I feel each drop you cry,
Just remember in you, you hold my life.

Please come to me and dry your tears,
There'll be no more crying, I'll ease your fears,
Just hold me close and don't let go,
I'll wipe those tears and protect your soul.

This Reality

Is this a dream or reality?
Something in my mind, come save me,
Searching for the answers, will I find?
Lost within eternity's confines.

Passions lustful burning desire,
Is it you who calls me to life?
Bleeding, my heart and soul want more,
Crying tears through your open door.

In minds confusion I lay awake,
Trapped like the serpent I forsake,
The darkness it haunts my dreams so long,
Never to let me awake from this song.

Immortal sins cloud my head,
Bring me back to life, wake me from dead,
This dream is not all it's to be,
Save me in time, don't let my heart bleed.

Clouds

"As she sits and waits,
Clouds encircle her body,
She feels the cold presence,
As she tries to grip her sanity"

Look at her, innocent child,
Encircled by loves passion, died,
Left to her torture she fills your desire,
Slowly crawling with the creatures inside.

Close your eyes to all around,
Breathe the air filled with clouds,
As you watch her fade away,
Extinguished by your loves pain.

You saw her in your head,
She'll take your life instead,
Leave your heart upon the ground,
Rip it out and feed the clouds.

As the clouds come to pass,
A body lays on the ground,
You can run to her and cry,
But it's too late, tears fill your eyes.

Now you sit and look to the sky,
Your body calling out why,
She took with her your heart,
Now left alone torn apart.

Immoral Soul

Will there be no one to hear my cries?
In the still of the night, my suicide,
Forsaken by this life's worst genocide,
I call out to thee, will you keep me alive?

Falling through chaos, it seems so alone,
I give my all to those, my life do they own?
Trapped by my own forgiving heart,
Bleeding me dry, they all start.

Compelled by my thoughts, I lead them astray,
Corrupting my soul, leading the way,
Lord hear my cries for in You I do believe,
The salvation in Your hands, today I plead.

Save my soul from the evil I do,
Blinded to those, if only they knew,
Hide all the pain, the guilt will follow,
Wishing my life to the ground it swallows.

I ask You for help, I need it right now,
This pain and obsession destroys me somehow,
Forgive all my sins, save me from the past,
I cry unto Thee, let my soul ever last.

I pour out my heart, I have nothing to hide,
You are my saviour, in You I confide,
I pray that one day, it'll all wash away,
But for now on my knees, do I sit here and pray.

Lord forgive me, and show me my strength,
The courage I need, for what I am meant,
The passion you seek from my immoral soul,
Please show me the way to make my life whole.

Passions Dying Heart

Where has all the passion gone,
My heart feels it's died,
I used to long for your embrace,
Now all is cold inside.

Where are all the feelings?
That used to feed my soul,
Replaced by something empty,
No longer to feel whole,

I can't believe there's nothing there,
No feeling any more,
There was a time I swore to you,
My love for you would soar.

I refuse to let it end this way,
I know there's more to give,
If I shall die in trying,
At least my life will live,

So time to find the passion,
Once more the war begins,
If this will be my last goodbye
I'll know we'll meet again.

Wanting...

I want to stand in the pouring rain,
and for me to cry your name,

I want the Earth to swallow me up,
and for it to feel my pain,

I want this life to be free,
and only spent with you.

I want the night and the day,
born in sun's morning dew.

I want to watch the sunrise,
while you lay there in my arms.

I want for me to bleed my soul,
and resist all your charm.

I want to feel me rise again,
so that I may see your face.

And lastly want to kiss your lips
and feel love's embrace.

Sorry

I only told you yesterday I loved you,
Today you threw it back without any sound,
I thought you said we'd make it better,
I didn't know a new love you found.

Can you remember how you loved me?
Those silly games we used to play,
Maybe sorry was not said often,
And only heartache left my way.

I know now only I'm the one to blame,
The mistakes I've done are now the past,
Damaged hearts beyond repair now,
No wonder my love's weren't meant to last.

All I can say now is I'm sorry,
Even now it seems too late,
I know sometimes it's hard to love me,
For now it's better without the hate.

What have we left to do?

Baby you stand there with my heart in your hand,
Darling put that knife away, I've always had a plan,
Just like we rehearsed now, though it seems so long ago,
Now it's all that we've got in this life it's time to let go.

I know life dealt us some unforeseen cards,
But tomorrow it'll all be a thing of the past,
So come take my hand in yours, for eternity's ever last,
Together we've still got a chance to set sail this ships mast.

It was so very long ago, since that night we first met,
Taking you to places, I fell into your net,
Tell me that tomorrow would bring more of the same,
But now it's come to this baby. It's all such a shame.

So tell me my sweetness what have we left to do?
You have a knife in your hand to cut me like a fool.
Is this the part where we say true love never dies?
So baby it's up to you now, Will I die or am I to survive?

Haunting Angel

Forgotten words.
Lost, like the torment of a lovers dead heart.
Misplaced in times effervescent mists.
Found only by desires.
Once passion burned.
Now the haunting has begun.
Death only the door.
Open for those whose hearts are pure.
Awaiting angels fallen to times lost grace.
Secretly waiting to fly again.
But dying to live a life.
Catch them as they fall.
In the hope that one day they'll be yours.
The fallen angel in your arms.
The haunting is no more.

Darkened Rain

Destroy something beautiful,
Have the world fall to it's knees,

Unleash hell's hidden fury,
Give her something to believe,

Caught in the dark skies,
Her soul doomed with mine

Forgotten time's stolen,
Drunk by poisoned wine,

Steal away the sunlight,
Let eternal darkness rain,

Come to me my baby,
We'll free ourselves again.

Sweet Will

Beaten down by life's sweet will, falling through the rain,
I sit here still, silently waiting for the end,
And right here and now it's where I'm at. About to face the truth,
Of who I am, and what I've done, and of my life's use.

Every second I spend without you,
My lungs draw endless breaths,
For without you my world is dying,
But I know that you are safe.

I Am My Own Man

Why in the hell are they looking at me?
What I say now is what I believe,
The press and the media built up this town,
Who the fuck are they cos I can pull it right down.

All the man made stars that entertain the world,
Who are they but media made fools?
Wait till you listen cos there's a new kid in town,
And no press or media can take this shit down.

Do they really think they know who I am?
What sort of person do they take for this man?
How many times do I have to say?
I am my own man and I like it that way.

They talk to me as if I'm their friend,
All people want from me is not to offend,
Those little boys and girls that look up to me,
They can go fuck themselves if you know what I mean.

Do they really think they know who I am?
What sort of person do they take for this man?
How many times do I have to say?
I am my own man and I like it that way.

Who gave them the right to interfere in my life?
My love life is mine and so is my wife
So any of you who want to know the real me
There is none, so ha! I am not reality

Cos do they really think they know who I am?
What sort of person do they take for this man?
How many times do I have to say?
I am my own man and I like it that way.

"And then I look up and see you standing there,
The only one who can make my eyes stare?
And my life so complete in every way,
I am my own man but would you like me to stay"

Cos do they really think they know who I am?
What sort of person do they take for this man?
How many times do I have to say?
I am my own man and I like it that way.

Poisoned Kiss

You think that I'm strong, yet I'm falling on my knees,
You said love was strong, yet it's crushing me so weak,
I think that I am drowning, into the waves of time,
So someone come and save me... cos I'm running out of rhyme...

I said before to you, that I'd always be so strong,
Then you came here, I found out I was wrong,
I felt you move me, in ways that I can't say,
And now I'm hurting, so please take me away.

And now all I can say is this, with a poisoned loving kiss.
And all my dreams somehow, turn to dust in time yet now,
You've captured my broken heart, but can you help it heal?
I long to see the day, the time when I can feel.

It feels so long now, since the day that you were mine,
And all this heartache, should've healed my blood like wine,
But nothing ever, seems to take the pain away,
Just thoughts of you, left for my dying day...

And now all I can say is this, with a poisoned loving kiss.
And all my dreams somehow, turn to dust in time yet now,
You've captured my broken heart, but can you help it heal?
I long to see the day, the time when I can feel.

Words Lost Meanings

'No more meaning do I have, I know it sounds absurd,
If you can find any, then please be my guest,
A cry for help, maybe, but leave me loneliness.'

Look into my soul and tell me what you see,
Lost inside myself for all to see,
Leave me this way for me to die,
Or give me some hope to discover my life.

Darkness once, just the absence of light,
A reflection of my soul, perhaps tonight,
Darkened by all the sins I have done,
Confessions for someone's life I've undone.

Look into my soul and tell me what you see,
Lost inside myself for all to see,
Leave me this way for me to die,
Or give me some hope to discover my life.

Look at me now with these words so plain,
I leave you nothing, but my life so vain,
Who knows one day I'll see the light,
But for now surrounded by darkness tonight.

Look into my soul and tell me what you see,
Lost inside myself for all to see,
Leave me this way for me to die,
Or give me some hope to discover my life.

Take Me Back

Leaving you was so hard to do,
It was something I never planned,
What happened to lead us to this point?
Please let me take your hand.

We've been through life's up and downs,
You were my queen, you wore my crown,
Please tell me that you'll take me back,
We can get our life back on track.

I never thought It'd end this way,
I feel so lonely inside,
Please forgive me for what I've done,
The pain will heal in time.

We've been through life's up and downs,
You were my queen, you wore my crown,
Please tell me that you'll take me back,
We can get our life back on track.

So long with you I got careless,
Work seemed to me more important,
And then it started, this cold war,
I put our life on hold, I never saw.

We've been through life's up and downs,
You were my queen, you wore my crown,
Please tell me that you'll take me back,
We can get our life back on track.

Please tell me we can make it through?
I promise I can change,
Give me that chance you know I need,
To redeem my hearts hard pain.

We've been through life's up and downs,
You were my queen, you wore my crown,
Please tell me that you'll take me back,
We can get our life back on track.

Love's Solitude

You ask me how I am, How I'm doing?
My life slowing dying, falling to oblivion,
I just need some hope, something to believe in,
Cast aside my fears and let's start living,

In my world of loves solitude,
Come save me, tell me what I'm to do?
Fooled by loves everlasting kiss,
It's my life, and you're all that I miss.

You talked to me so softly, my heart so tender,
Now all that's left is gone from here,
Give me that sign, I need it so bad,
I want to start living, the life that I had.

In my world of loves solitude,
Come save me, tell me what I'm to do?
Fooled by loves everlasting kiss,
It's my life, and you're all that I miss.

In my world of loves solitude,
Come save me, tell me what I'm to do?
Fooled by loves everlasting kiss,
It's my life, and you're all that I miss.

Gone Away

I got out of bed this morning, just to see your breaking smile,
I told you how it's alright, I'll be here for a while,
I went to make you breakfast, but it was then I really knew,
My eyes deceived to find you and so my thoughts were true.

You didn't let me know you were leaving,
I would have begged for you to stay,
I now lay here, my heart bleeding,
Cos it's too late, you've gone away..
You've gone away..

If I knew you were to leave me, would I have changed my life style?
Would I have been more attentive, caught that look up in your eyes?
Would I have told you how much I loved you, with all my heart and soul?
Could I change your minds impression, would you accept me as your whole?

You didn't let me know you were leaving,
I would have begged for you to stay,
I now lay here, my heart bleeding,
Cos it's too late, you've gone away..
You've gone away..

You didn't let me know you were leaving,
I would have begged for you to stay,
I now lay here, my heart bleeding,
Cos it's too late, You've gone away..
You've gone away..

God I miss you so much.
Your every move, your smile, your touch,
Please tell me you'll come back to me,
I can't take it, it's too much.

Lay Here

I never thought it would come to this,
We both knew that we'd be missed.
So now that we're on our own,
Tell me how far we both should go?

You said you love your man,
And I said I love my girl,
So what brings us to this time alone?

If my conscience would allow,
Would your conscience show me how?
But we both know each other better,
This loves just like the weather.

Could I take you from your man?
Could you take me from my girl?
I think we both know how far this thing could go,
Tell me you're in love with him,
I'll tell you I'm in love with her,
Then maybe we could fool each other.

Let me take you by the hand,
We can lay upon the sand,
And stay here for eternity.

You want to be with me
And I want to be with you,
Can life not make it that simple?

You tell me he's your man,
I tell you she's my girl,
And so we lay here in our shadow.

If I couldn't be with you,
And you couldn't be with me,
Tell me how do we end this thing now?
Cos girl I want you bad,
And I know that he's your man,
But don't tell me that it has to be this sad?

If you want to be with me,
Then girl lets just lay here in the sand,

You said you love your man,
And I said I love my girl,
So what brings us to this time alone?

www.ingramcontent.com/pod-product-compliance
Lightning Source LLC
Chambersburg PA
CBHW021013090426
42738CB00007B/770